Stickers!

An Activity Book

Where should you put the stickers? Wherever you decide!

Decorate this white duck.

Do you like him in this outfit?

How about this one?

Use your imagination and go wild!

Invent, improvise, imagine, create, and when you're done, you will have made a book that is unique!

● It's also fun to draw after you place the stickers!

I could use
a little color here!

Good start, but I still
need something!

Perfect!
I look awesome!

● It's easy to find the perfect sticker.

The stickers in this book are sorted by color so you can tell what stickers we thought might be fun to use in each section. The colors of the square corner of the page and the sticker section at the back of the book will be the same.

Page

Stickers

1

1

This mouse has

This mouse has a candle.

Should the other mice have candles, too?

Hurry hurry!

Where do you think they're all going?

It's a birthday party! What a beautiful cake!
Could you help them put the candles on it?

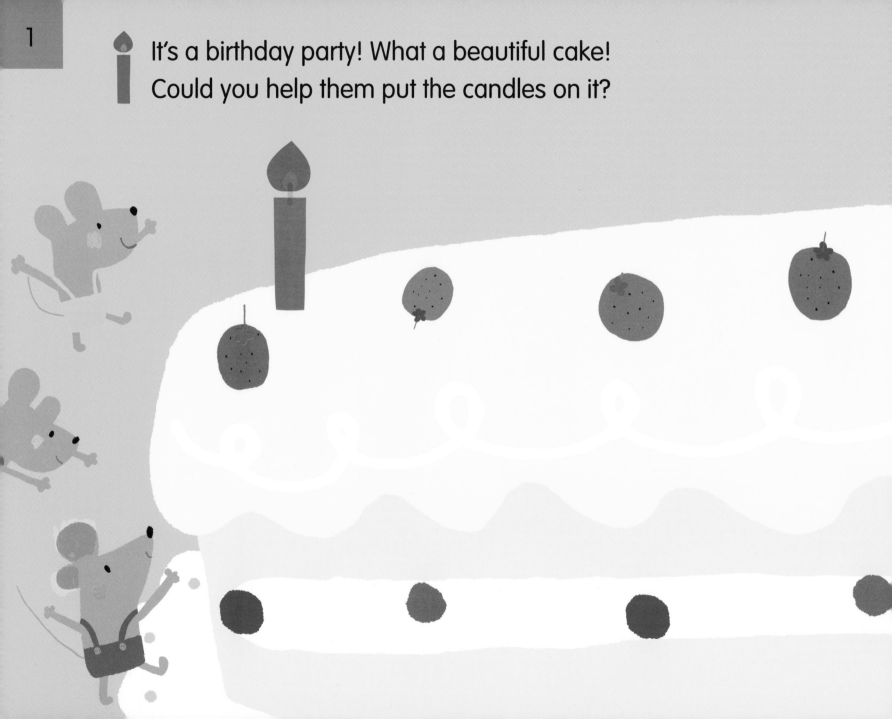

How else can you decorate the birthday cake?

Pancakes for everyone!

The chef has made
a gigantic pancake!
There's enough for everyone.
Come and get it!

Everyone wants some of the pancake!
Can you put some on their plates?

Let's give some to the octopus, too.

He'll start with eight pieces!

Can I have some, please?

Everyone wants to get moving!

How can they get around without feet?
Maybe wheels would help.

Vroom vroom vroom…

Let's give everything wheels! The flowers are already rolling.
How about the fish? The tree? This cake has a party to get to!

Vroooom…

Let's get everyone rolling!
Add some wheels.

Vrooom…

Draw a road for them to drive on!

No one wants to be left out.
Let's give everything wheels!

Do you think these ducks are cute?

They certainly think so!
Colored leaves have
fallen into the water.
The ducks want to use them
to make a fashion show.

Don't you love my hat?

Look at me!

What else can you give them to wear?

What kind of outfits can we make with leaves?
Let's help them look stylish.

How cool am I?

I look great, right?

 More leaves have fallen into the water.

The fish want to have a fashion show, too.

Let's help them out.

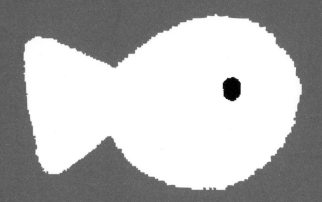

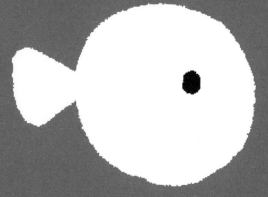

Aren't skirts wonderful?

Everyone wants to wear one!

How do I look?

Let's choose skirts that look good on everyone.

Who else wants a skirt?

Can you draw a ribbon for my hair?

What else can you draw to dress up the flowers?

Oh my,
that's funny!

How does lipstick look on me?

Let's put lipstick on everyone.

What else can you give them?
Hats? Neckties? Use your imagination!

Should I wear lipstick?

How do I look?

Oh my,
you look good.

Now everybody wants some!

Me too! Me too!

Goo! Goo!

The silly ghosts all agree: They want some lipstick, too!

Make me look pretty, please!

I could use a little color.

Also available from Seven Footer Kids:

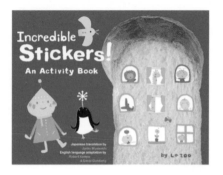

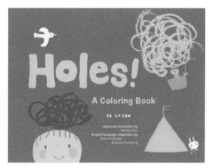

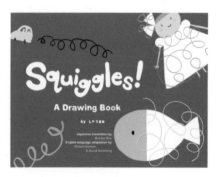

The King of Play Book "Odekakekun: Ure-Seal Tano-Seal"
© 2006 La ZOO / GAKKEN
First published in Japan 2006 by Gakken Co., Ltd., Tokyo
English translation rights arranged with Gakken Education
Publishing Co., Ltd. through Nextoy, LLC

Published by Seven Footer Kids, an imprint of Seven Footer Press,
a division of Seven Footer Entertainment LLC, NY
Manufactured in Shenzhen, Guangdong, P.R.China
in 03/2010 by C&C Offset Printing Co.
10 9 8 7 6 5 4 3 2
© Copyright Seven Footer Kids, 2010 for English Edition
All Rights Reserved
English adaptation designed by Junko Miyakoshi

ISBN 978-1-934734-37-7

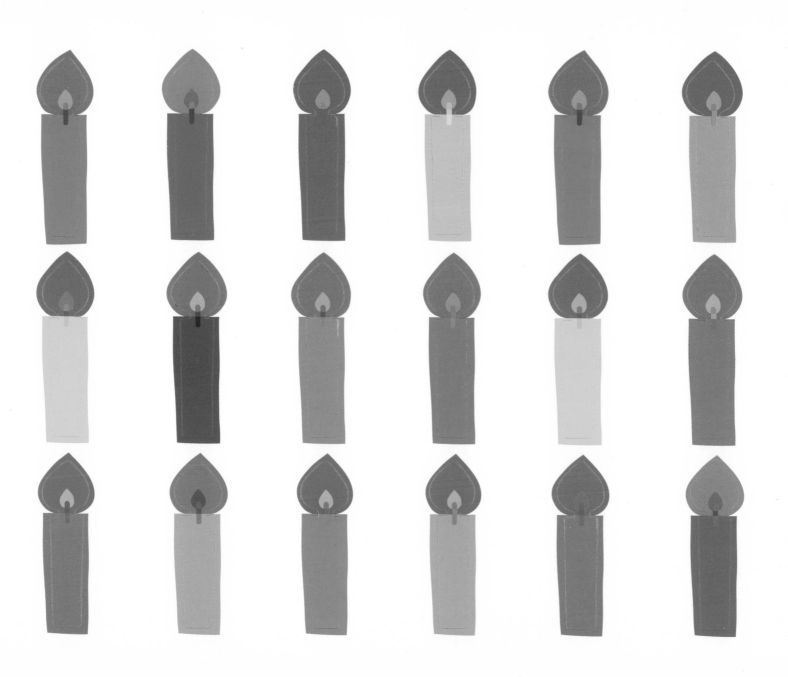

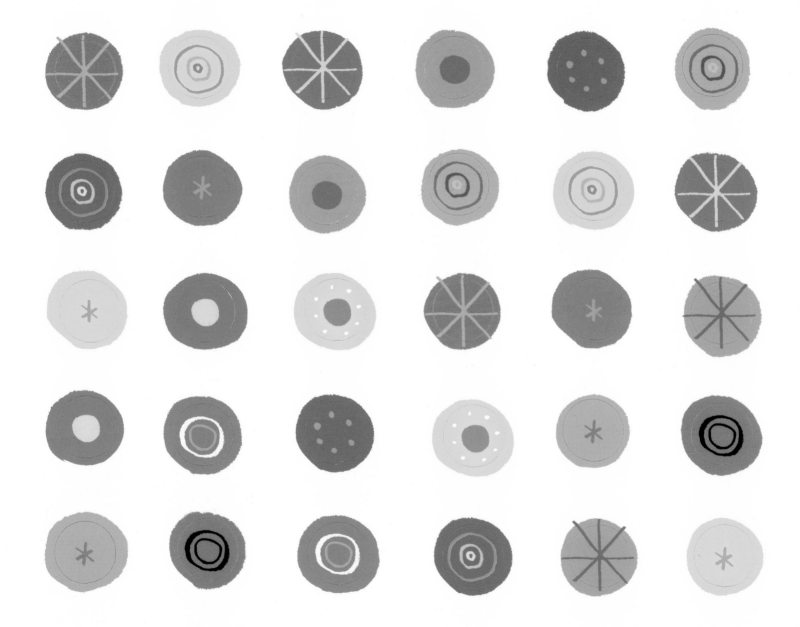